SHEPHERDS

for
Dr Lloyd

Thank you for
caring for so many
" lambs! "

Terry & Jan's
Walker

Books by Janis Walker

ALLELUIA! A GOSPEL DIARY

FIRST READING: A DIARY

HALLELUJAH! A PSALM RESPONSE DIARY

SECOND READING: A DIARY

A TRIP TO GRACE

SHEPHERDS

MYSTERY!

SHEPHERDS

by

Janis Walker

Pallium Press

lovingly

dedicated

to

all

shepherds

Jesus said, "I am the good shepherd. I know my own and my own know me, just as the Father knows me and I know the Father. And I lay down my life for the sheep. I have other sheep that do not belong to this fold. I must bring them also, and they will listen to my voice. So there will be one flock, one shepherd."

(John 10, 14-16 NRSV)

Scripture quotations marked BCP are from The Book of Common Prayer, 1789, 1979.

Scripture quotations marked RSV are from The Revised Standard Version of the Bible, copyright 1952 [2nd edition, 1971] by the Division of Christian Education of the National Council of the Churches of Christ in the United States of America. Used by permission. All rights reserved.

Scripture quotations marked NRSV are from The New Revised Standard Version, copyright © 1989, Division of Christian education of the National Council of the Churches of Christ in the United States of America. Reprinted by Permission.

Scripture quotations marked KJV are from The King James Version of the bible.

Every effort has been made to insure accuracy of text and quotations, and any errors or omissions brought to our attention will be corrected in future editions.

SECOND PRINTING 2016

Pallium Press, P.O. Box 60910, Palo Alto, CA 94306-0910
We regret that Pallium Press cannot accept or return unsolicited manuscripts.

Check for new titles by Janis Walker at www.palliumpress.com

Pallium Press books are available at www.Amazon.com, www.BarnesandNoble.com, or at your favorite local bookstore.

cover photos: Terry Walker - San Francisco and Giverny, France
cover design: Janis Walker

Copyright © 2016 by Janis Walker

Printed in the United States of America.

ISBN 978-0-9826883-2-8

Acknowledgments

Thank you to Terry and Christopher! You have always loved me and supported me on this mysterious journey of "a long obedience in the same direction."

Thank you to the community of St. Patrick's Seminary past and present, especially the extra-ordinary Class of 1991.

Thank you to the Jesuit priests from the Jesuit Retreat Center in Los Altos, especially those who have been my spiritual directors. I am forever grateful to you.

Thank you to the Rev. Richard Leslie, who was my wonderful Field Education supervisor when I was an Episcopalian. I am very grateful to Richard and to many others for their understanding, encouragement, and support over so many years. I pray to be worthy of your trust.

Thank you to the Rev. Dr. Carlton Young, our holy and wise supervisor in Clinical Pastoral Education. Our very exuberant group had fun quoting Mrs. Maisy Young, who warned Carlton, "Don't try that CPE stuff on ME!"

I am always grateful for the memory of the late Rev. Dr. Peter Marshall (the "Dominie"), the

Scottish minister who became the Chaplain of the U.S. Senate. Catherine Marshall's book, <u>A Man Called Peter,</u> was one of the strong influences in my early life and interest in ministry. It was a privilege a few years ago to meet the Rev. Peter John Marshall, son of Peter and Catherine.

I am enormously grateful for the writing of Agnes Sanford. Her books, especially <u>Lost Shepherd</u>, <u>The Healing Light,</u> and <u>Behold Your God,</u> have taught me a great deal about healing and about intercessory prayer. In the summer of 1989, Terry and I visited Trinity Episcopal Church in Moorestown, New Jersey, where Agnes and her husband, the Rev. Ted Sanford, lived when Ted was the Rector. It meant so much to me to pray in the little chapel where Agnes prayed.

A.M.D.G.

22 February 2012

"The LORD is my shepherd; I shall not want.
He maketh me to lie down in green pastures:
he leadeth me beside the still waters.
He restoreth my soul:
he leadeth me in the paths of righteousness
for his name's sake.
Yea, though I walk through
the valley of the shadow of death,
I will fear no evil: for thou art with me;
thy rod and thy staff they comfort me.
Thou preparest a table before me
in the presence of my enemies:
thou anointest my head with oil;
my cup runneth over.
Surely goodness and mercy shall follow me
all the days of my life:
and I shall dwell in the house of
the LORD for ever (Psalm 23, KJV)."

Part I   Good Shepherd Sunday in 1994

When I was an Episcopalian, I preached in two different parishes on the fourth Sunday of Easter, Good Shepherd Sunday (Vocation Sunday). The Gospel for this particular homily, in April, 1994, was John 10, 11-18.

Jesus said, "I am the good shepherd. The good shepherd lays down his life for the sheep. The hired hand, who is not the shepherd and does not own the sheep, sees the wolf coming and leaves the sheep and runs away – and the wolf snatches them and scatters them. The hired hand runs away because a hired hand does not care for the sheep. I am the good shepherd. I know my own and my own know me, just as the Father knows me and I know the Father. And I lay down my life for the sheep. I have other sheep that do not belong to this fold. I must bring them also, and they will listen to my voice. So there will be one flock, one shepherd. For this reason the Father loves me, because I lay down my life in order to take it up again. No one takes it from me, but I lay it down of my own accord. I have power to lay it down, and I have power to take it up again. I have received this command from my Father (John 10, 11-18 NRSV)."

THE SHEPHERD

"Shepherd of souls, refresh and bless
thy chosen pilgrim flock
with manna in the wilderness,
with water from the rock."

Hymn 343, The Hymnal 1982 (St. Agnes)

Since early childhood, I have loved lambs! Mother baked my birthday cakes in the shape of lambs. I remember a trip to White Sands, New Mexico, as a small child. There was a gift shop and I remember a small white ceramic lamb.

All through our home there are lambs (Gianna and others), pictures of shepherdesses in blue and their lambs, lamb candlesticks, and cards of lambs sent from friends.

I am very grateful for a beautiful stained-glass window of the Agnus Dei, the Lamb of God, which Terry designed and made for me. Christopher, a child at the time, helped with this project. Terry and I took this window to a little chapel I love and a priest friend blessed it on the altar.

Once in England, when Christopher was eleven, we were going to lunch, in Oxfordshire, at the "Maytime." Across the meadow were lambs peacefully grazing. I called out "Baaa baaa," not really expecting a response. To our amazement, the whole flock came bleating over see to us, right up close!

A friend in Sonoma County, Marcia, once named one of her newborn lambs after me! I was very honored.

Today I want to tell you about a lamb who became a shepherd and about a shepherd who became a lamb. A dual vocation.

John's Gospel tells us of John the Baptist, whose ministry it was to prepare the way of the Lord. John the Baptist looked at Jesus and told the people, "Behold the Lamb of God, who takes away the sin of the world (John 1:29 RSV)"!

This is what we, as baptized Christians, are called to do. We are called to point to Jesus the Lamb and to proclaim by word and example the Good News of God in Christ.

In the Old Testament days, the people knew all about the importance of the lamb of sacrifice. You remember, in the very first Passover, the Lord told Moses and Aaron to instruct the people to take a lamb, a lamb without blemish, slaughter it, put the blood on the door posts and lintel of the house, then roast the lamb and eat it. According to Exodus 12,

"The blood shall be a sign for you on the houses where you live: when I see the blood, I will pass over you, and no plague shall destroy you … (Exodus 12:13 NRSV)."

We may shudder and turn away from the notion of blood. But to these ancient people, blood was essential. According to the book of Leviticus, "For the life of the flesh is in the blood; and I have given it for you for making atonement for your lives on the altar; for, as life, it is the blood that makes atonement (Leviticus 17:11 NRSV)."

In the New Testament, the writer of the book of Hebrews tells us, "Indeed, under the law almost everything is purified with blood, and without the shedding of blood there is no forgiveness of sins (Hebrews 9:22 NRSV)."

We're beginning to see why Jesus shed his blood on the Cross to take away our sins. The animal sacrifices of the Old Testament happened over and over. Jesus shed his precious blood once and for all.

According to the writer to the Hebrews, " … how much more will the blood of Christ, who through the eternal Spirit offered himself without blemish to God, purify our conscience from dead works to worship the living God (Hebrews 9:14 NRSV)!"

Rightly do we proclaim that Christ our Passover is sacrificed for us. He IS our Passover Lamb.

We have seen Jesus as the Lamb of God who became the Good Shepherd, who was sacrificed for our sake. We turn now to an earthly shepherd who became a lamb of sacrifice.

This is a true story from World War II. A Polish priest, a Franciscan, Fr. Maximillian Kolbe, now a canonized saint, was 45 years old when the Nazis invaded his country in the autumn of 1939. He lived in a community of some 700 priests and monks. They were taken to the prison camp of Amtitz, where they ministered to others in the power of the Holy Spirit.

Fr. Kolbe was then taken to Auschwitz in l941. Charles Colson, in his 1992 book <u>The Body</u>, has written movingly of Fr. Kolbe.

One day in July a prisoner managed to escape. To retaliate, the guards sent ten prisoners to the dreaded starvation bunker. One man on the way to his death began to weep for his wife and children. Father Kolbe began to call for the commandant and offered his own life in place of the weeping man.

As Mr. Colson, writes, "For the first and last time, the commandant looked Fr. Kolbe in the eye. 'Who are you?' he asked. 'I am a Catholic priest.'" The commandant drew a line through the first prisoner's number, #5659, and instead wrote down Fr. Kolbe's number, #16670.

"Past prisoners had spent their dying days howling, attacking one another, clawing the walls in a frenzy of despair. But now, coming from the death box, those outside heard the faint sounds of singing. For this time the prisoners had a shepherd to gently lead them through the valley of the shadow of death, pointing them to the Great Shepherd. And perhaps for that reason Father Kolbe was the last to die."(Chapter 23 "Who Are You?" in The Body, 1992, by Charles Colson).

Today, let us ask ourselves two questions. As a lamb, am I trusting in Jesus, my Shepherd, to lead me in the way he thinks is best for me?

It has been said, "The Shepherd knows what pastures are best for his sheep, and they must not question nor doubt, but trustingly follow Him. Perhaps he sees that the best pastures for some of us are to be found in the midst of opposition or of earthly trials. If He leads you there, you may be sure they are green for you, and you will grow strong by feeding there. Perhaps He sees that the best waters for you to walk beside will be raging waters of trouble and sorrow. If that should be the case, He will make them still waters for you, and you must go and lie down beside them... (Mrs. H.W.S., Daily Strength for Daily Needs, by Mary W. Tillotson, 1884). As lambs, we must learn to trust our Shepherd."

The second question: "As a shepherd, am I laying down my life for the lambs entrusted to my care?" The Scottish New Testament scholar, Dr. William Barclay, has written of two dangers to the Church.

According to Dr. Barclay, the Church " ... is always liable to trouble from outside, from the wolves and the robbers and the marauders. It is always liable to trouble from the inside, from the false shepherd. The Church runs a double danger. It is always under attack from outside, and often suffers from the tragedy of bad leadership, from the disaster of shepherds who see their calling as a career and not as a means of service.

"The second danger is by far the worse, because, if the shepherd is faithful and good, there is a strong defense from the attack from the outside; but if the shepherd is faithless and a hireling, the foes from outside can penetrate into and destroy the flock. The Church's first essential is a leadership based on the example of Jesus Christ (The Daily Bible Study Series, The Gospel of John, Vol. 2 Revised Edition, pp.62-63)."

You may not think you are a leader or a shepherd, but as a baptized Christian living in this dark world, the light of Christ shines through you. You are called to make Christ known in your home, your work, your school, and yes, in the Church. You are strategically placed there by God.

Please pray with me. Maybe you believe in God, but God doesn't seem real to you, even though you've gone to church for years. Maybe God is very real to you, but you are struggling with a problem and feel completely boxed in. God already has the solution. What He wants you to do is to trust and obey Him.

Lord Jesus, thank you for being my Lamb and my Savior. Thank you for dying on the Cross for me and for forgiving me. Help me to forgive all who have hurt me.

Lord Jesus, thank you for being my Shepherd and my Lord. Thank you for leading me in the way you think best. Thank you for being my Good Shepherd and holding me close to your heart. I give to you now the situation that is troubling me. I trust you to work it out. Show me the next step you want me to take. Help me to trust you and obey you in this matter.

"And so, to him to sits upon the throne,
and to Christ the Lamb,
Be worship and praise, dominion and
splendor,
for ever and for evermore."

(Canticle 18, "Song to the Lamb,"
Book of Common Prayer)

Amen.

Part II   Reflections about Jesus, our Good Shepherd

A. Jesus, our Good Shepherd, was born a Jew!

Sometimes we forget that Jesus, our Good Shepherd, was Jewish! St. Paul, apostle to the Gentiles, reminds us of this in Romans 11, in his vivid imagery of the olive tree and the wild olive shoot which has been grafted.

St. Paul also reminds us "As many of you as were baptized into Christ have clothed yourselves with Christ. There is no longer Jew or Greek, there is no longer slave or free, there is no longer male or female; for you are all one in Christ Jesus. And if you belong to Christ, then you are Abraham's offspring, heirs according to the promise (Galatians 3, 27-29 NRSV)."

In April, 1985, I was so happy to be on pilgrimage in Israel. Our group, led by the late Rev. Brad Hall, was based at St. George's Anglican College in Jerusalem.

Later, that summer, Terry and Christopher and I went to Texas for a family reunion on my mother's side. Mother's cousin, a Methodist minister, studied family history and organized these wonderful summer reunions.

There was a surprise this time. I learned that my great-grandmother's maiden name was COHEN! I felt deeply comforted and full of joy, having always had a love for the Jewish people.

Several years ago, our parish visited a nearby synagogue for a great kosher dinner and a presentation by the rabbi. Someone asked him about the Messiah. Gently, the rabbi said, "You believe he has already come. We are still waiting for him. Let us wait together."

B. Jesus, our Good Shepherd, is our Great High Priest who intercedes for us.

In his April 24, 2005, inaugural homily, Pope Benedict XVI spoke eloquently of Jesus as our Shepherd. The new Pope noted that the pallium was the first symbol of papal ministry. He said, "The symbolism of the pallium is even more concrete: the lamb's wool is meant to represent the lost, sick or weak sheep which the shepherd places on his shoulders and carries to the waters of life. For the Fathers of the Church, the parable of the lost sheep which the shepherd seeks in the desert, was an image of the mystery of Christ and the Church. The human race – every one of us – is the sheep lost in the desert, which no longer knows the way. The Son of God will not let this happen; he cannot abandon humanity in so wretched a condition. He leaps to his feet and abandons the glory of heaven, in order to go in search of the sheep and pursue it, all the way to the Cross. He takes it upon his shoulders and carries our humanity; he carries us all – he is the good shepherd who lays down his life for the sheep." (Pope Benedict XVI, April 24, 2005)

Jesus is our priest forever. Jesus " … holds his priesthood permanently, because he continues forever. Consequently he is able for all time to save those approach God through him, since he always lives to make intercession for them (Hebrews 7, 24, 25 NRSV)." He is " … our great high priest who has passed through the heavens, Jesus, the Son of God (Hebrews 4, 14 NRSV)."

C. Jesus, our Good Shepherd, is the great example of how to care for his flock

In the fall of 2011, I came across the book, Christ – The Ideal of the Priest by The Rt. Rev. D. Columba Marmion (Dom Marmion) of Maredous Abbey. The book, based on conferences given to priests, was published in 1952, and has timeless insights into living one's vocation as a shepherd of souls.

Referring to Pentecost, Dom Marmion stated, "From this moment, the Church, in spite of persecutions, of disputes about doctrine, in spite of the faithlessness of her own children, has lived and triumphed in a wondrous manner. She is always one in her faith and in her allegiance to the see of Peter; at all times she produces sanctity in her members by virtue of her own sanctifying power; she includes, as of right, the whole human race in her sheepfold … (page 261)."

Part III   Shepherds in Fiction

Two characters in books by English novelist, Elizabeth Goudge, seem very real to me. I read these books many years ago and still occasionally re-read them.

Hilary Eliot, the Anglican vicar, in <u>Pilgrims's Inn</u>, was sixty-six, " ... a bachelor country parson ... who looked already an old man. Yet he had the Eliot charm ... a complete lack of affectation, a simplicity that was wholly disarming and yet a little misleading, because it was combined with considerable astuteness ... Hilary's kind brown eyes saw a very great deal more that most people realized .... And he had, too, a charm that was all his own, an indefinable air of aristocracy that was the outcome of his own secret spiritual victories. In Hilary that something in a man that is independent of inheritance, training, or tradition ... had grown to unusual height and strength."

In another of Elizabeth Goudge's novels, <u>The Scent of Water</u>, there is the eccentric "old vicar" who was staying at the vicarage while the Vicar was away on holiday. The "old" vicar had ministered in London slums and had keen insight into the human condition. The distressed young Mary wrote of him in her diary, "I told him everything. It was the queerest thing that ever happened to me because I take such infinite

17

trouble to cover it all up. And yet here I was laying it all out in front of him." After their conversation, the old vicar "held out his right hand to me. I held it and it was dry and rough and hot. 'My dear,' he said, 'I will pray for you every day of my life until I die.'" "'My dear,' he said, 'love, your God, is a trinity. There are three necessary prayers and they have three words each. They are these, 'Lord, have mercy. Thee I adore. Into thy hands.' Not difficult to remember. If in times of distress you hold to these you will do well.'"

Part IV Shepherd's Pie

Here are two places to try, if you are in California in the San Francisco Bay Area and would like a Shepherd's Pie. There are sure to be many other places also.

The first is Pelican Inn (it looks very 16th century English) at Muir Beach north of San Francisco. They just have it at lunch, I think. Go to their web site and see the fireplace. There is a recreation of a "Priest Hole" where priests could hide when Catholic priests in England were being martyred. The words over the fireplace are "Fear Knocked at the door. Faith answered. No one was there."

The second is in Palo Alto at the Rose and Crown Pub downtown. They have a nice web site also. We just get fish and chips there and have not had the Shepherd's Pie.

If you would like to make one yourself, there are many recipes for both traditional and vegetarian Shepherd's Pie in cookbooks and online. They are easy to make and lots of fun. It is especially good to use Golden Yukon potatoes for the mashed potatoes on top.

Part V Conclusion

We began in the tenth chapter of the Gospel of John and that is where we conclude, with the Lord's determination to have one flock.

"I am the good shepherd. I know my own and my own know me, just as the Father knows me and I know the Father. And I lay down my life for the sheep. I have other sheep that do not belong to this fold. I must bring them also, and they will listen to my voice. So there will be one flock, one shepherd (John 10, 14-16 NRSV)."

Let us pray together. "Now may the God of peace, who brought back from the dead our Lord Jesus, the great shepherd of the sheep, by the blood of the eternal covenant, make you complete in everything good so that you may do his will, working among us that which is pleasing in his sight, through Jesus Christ, to whom be the glory forever and ever. Amen (Hebrews 13, 20-21 NRSV)."

in loving memory

of

Blessed Father Jerzy Popieluszko
(<u>Do You Hear the Bells, Father Jerzy?</u>)

and

The Cistercian Monks of Tibhirine
("Des Hommes et Des Dieux")

Please pray for us to be given the strength
to stay the course.

Janis Walker is the author of <u>Alleluia! A Gospel Diary</u> and <u>A Trip to Grace</u>. In 1991, she received her M.A. Theology degree from St. Patrick's Seminary. Her thesis director was the late Rev. Frank Norris, S.S., a translator for the ecumenical observers at the Second Vatican Council. Fr. Norris was her sponsor, along with Mrs. Ann Masik, R.N., when she was received into the Roman Catholic Church May 13, 1998, in a Chrism Mass for Christian Unity in Rossi Chapel at the Jesuit Retreat Center in Los Altos. She and her husband are currently planning a trip to Texas in the spring to visit family, friends, and to see the bluebonnets.